A Colorful
LEGACY

*(Artwork, African Proverbs and
Words of Inspiration)*

Illustrated & Written by
Terry Tabor

Archway Publishing books may be ordered through booksellers or by contacting:

Archway Publishing
1663 Liberty Drive
Bloomington, IN 47403
www.archwaypublishing.com
844-669-3957

Psalms 1:3

ISBN: 978-1-6657-4016-6 (sc)
ISBN: 978-1-6657-4017-3 (e)

Library of Congress Control Number: 2023904277

Print information available on the last page.

Archway Publishing rev. date: 06/29/2023

Endorsements

I am in awe of the wonderful talent and soothed with calmness by the wisdom of the African Proverbs. I'm so proud of Artist, Terry Tabor
LaKei ForestCosby, Photographer &
Treasurer, Sisters 4 Sisters Network, Inc.

Inspiring and mind blowing art and words of wisdom. However this is not surprising because it comes from an Inspiring artist such as yourself
Shirley and Fred Lathern Jr.
Former CGCS Co-worker and friend

Terry has given us a beautiful book of images she created that support the proverbs shown with them. I had connections with her art and the words on each page. The book should be shared with young and old of all race.
James Bray,
Bray Consultant

"Terry's creativity and 'one of a kind art' is literally breathtaking!"
Sharon J. Bullock
Visionary Author, "Embracing My Sexy Sixties!"

"A beautiful cross section of legacy meets artful purpose; this book showcases brilliant work from a soul that has seen the eyes of our Heavenly Father. Terry Tabor, you have crafted a lovely share that will undoubtedly inspire generations to come!"
Niquelle L. Cotton
CEO, Q-factor Consulting LLC

"Beautiful, Inspiring, Uplifting, the 3 W's Wonderful Words of Wisdom"
Wyomme Pariss, An Aesthete, Producer

Summary

My artwork throughout the years has a spiritual positive message. An artbook of positive titles with African Proverbs to reminisce on statements you may have heard while growing up from your grandparents, great grands, parents or just someone older giving you words of wisdom to help you throughout your life. This book is meant to bring back memories and a conversation piece from adults to our younger kids. Something that can be carried on to generations. A colorful table top book filled with artwork and encouraging words.

I wish that my artwork and words of encouragement can help empower a person to move forward in the right direction. Know you can do anything as long as you have faith.

Terry Tabor

Terry Tabor, a mixed medium artist. Silk Painting Artist that hand paints and dyes on silk for frame wall art and one-of-a-kind silk wearables. She also paints on canvas using mixed mediums.

Terry was born in Alexandria, VA in 1955 and currently resides in Maryland. She is a self-taught mixed medium artist who began drawing at an early age.

She inherited her artistic talent from her father, Lee E. Tabor, Sr., who was also an artist in his own right. Her father was creative and love making things out of wood. As well as her mother Johnnie Mae Holmes Tabor, a seamstress, cook and advisor on life. Most of all they were the friendliest persons she ever known.

She studied Silk Painting at Harmony Hall Regional Center in Fort Washington, MD under Diane Tuckman. Later, she attended various silk painting classes and workshops in the DMV area. In 2014 until 2018, Terry became the President of Silk Painters International Network, Inc. Local Chapter in MD. During that time, she started her Silk Painting Business, "Expressions by Terry", that shares the experience of making magic on silk through offering private lessons for beginners' silk painting and Design It Yourself private silk scarves parties the fun and easy way.

Terry traveled to West Africa and Hawaii where she felt the spirit through images in trees. The Spirit spoke to her and gave her a style of painting on silk with a message to the viewers on living life in a positive way. From the root to the branches; trees shape themselves to give messages. Whether they need sunlight or water; there are other messages to pay attention to.

This book shares Terry's interpretations of the messages from a Tree and other artwork with words of positive motivation quotes and African Proverbs.

ENJOY!!

Thanks to

Thanks to God in blessing me with a talent and the love
for painting on silk. Thank you for allowing me to spread
the inspiration to my grandkids and others.
Thanks to my two grandchildren (Ryanne Mone' and Tre) in
finding my drawing pad that I use to draw in to pass the time
away. At that time, I hadn't seen it in over 25 years.
Thanks to my youngest granddaughter Alaya for wanting to do arts and
crafts with me. A very memorable time that I will cherish forever.
Thanks to my daughter Anneka (Nikki) for her love and believing in me.
Thanks to Sandra Fleming in introducing me to Kevin Hicks from Annie's
Art Gallery. He was the first to display my artwork in his gallery.
Thanks to my family (Belinda, Tony, Barbara, Romaine, Ronnie, Diane, Angie,
Chauncia, Linder, Lois, Kelvin, LaTonga, Kisha & my dear sweetheart Jesse)
for their love and support. There is nothing like a close supporting family.
Thanks to my Sisters' by Heart (Karen, LaKei, Lonnie, Sandra & Sharon)
for always being there and giving me words of encouragement.
Thanks to my dear close friends and repeated customers/supporters (Alisa,
Barbara, Belinda, Beverly, Brenda, Bob, Candice, Carol, Carolyn, Denise,
Elena, Gary, Gloria, Hengie, Henny, Jackie, James, Jeanette, Jennifer, Jesse,
Joann, Joyce, Judy, Leslie, Michelle, Nikki, Paulette, Pat, Peggy, Phyllis,
Ray, Renee, Rickie, Robin, Sandra, Sharon, Shirley, Stephanie, Susan, Teri,
Tonya, Yvonne: just to name a few) in giving me unceasing support.

If I missed your name; please forgive me.

Without God, family and friends, I Could Not --- Can Not-- do any of this.
I LOVE YOU and appreciate you so much!!!!!!!!

May God continue to bless you and your families with
love, peace and good health.

A very special Thanks to Marian Thomas:
M & M Photography Expressions
In taking such beautiful pictures for the book

Terry Tabor

Name of Artwork: *7 Rules for Life*
Medium: *Oil on Canvas*

And he shall be like a tree planted by the rivers of water, that bringeth forth his fruit in his season: his leaf also shall not wither; and whatsoever he doeth shall prosper.

Psalm 1:3

Be Like A Tree

Stand Tall and Be Strong
Go out on a Limb
Remember your Roots
Drink Plenty of Water
Enjoy the Sunlight
Go with the Flow
Give to Others
Be Content with Natural Beauty
Show your True Colors
Get Along with Others
Take Time Alone
Be Different
Enjoy the View
Make Something of Yourself.

By Terry Tabor

Name of Artwork: Colorful Legacy II
Artwork: size: 17 x 21
Medium: Silk

In order to learn to grow and be happy, you must seek the new. Take a new route. Make some changes in your life. Do something different.

Terry Tabor

Artwork Title: Grow No Matter What
Artwork Size: 16 x 20
Artwork Medium: Acrylic

Put forth the effort and practically anything you desire is yours.
You and only you are accountable for what you do with your life.

African Proverbs

Artwork Title: Stand Tall
Artwork Size: 16 x 20
Artwork Medium: Silk

Strick while the fire is hot.

African Proverbs

Artwork Title: A Colorful Sound
Artwork Size: 12 x 36
Artwork Medium: Acrylic on canvas

Like branches on a tree; we may grow in different directions;
yet we are from the same root.

Terry Tabor

Artwork Title: Lady Love
Artwork Size: 20 x 24
Artwork Medium: Acrylic with Gold Leaves

The strongest light is the light that shines within you.
Use it to lead you in the direction of your Soul Purpose.

Unknown

Artwork Title: Loving Africa
Artwork Size: 22 x 28
Artwork Medium: Acrylic with Gold Leaf

Blood is thicker than water

African Proverb

Artwork Title: Sister's Keeper
Artwork Size: 24 x 36
Artwork Medium: Acrylic

It is Ok to be afraid but don't allow it to overcome what you want.

Terry Tabor

Artwork Title: Do It Afraid
Artwork Size: 30 x 40
Artwork Medium: Paint on Silk

What your head doesn't understand, your feet have to stand.

African Proverbs

Artwork Title: Fighting with Self
Artwork Size: 16 x 20
Artwork Medium: Acrylic Pouring Paint on Canvas

Imagination is just the start of a new idea, just act on it.
Try, try, try, try, try.
Never give up.

Terry Tabor

Artwork Title: Moving Forward
Artwork Size: 23 x 37
Artwork Medium: Acrylic on canvas

You are not falling apart.
You are falling into place.
Allow things to fall off.
Let them go so you can grow.

Unknown

Artwork Title: I'm Coming Out
Artwork Size: 16 x 20
Artwork Medium: Acrylic on canvas

Everyone has a gift and purpose.
Find yours.

Unknown

Artwork Title: My Fairy
Artwork Size: 18 x 24
Artwork Medium: Acrylic

Forgive and move on because two wrongs don't make a right.

African Proverbs

Artwork Title: In the Blue
Artwork Size: 16 x 20
Artwork Medium: Acrylic on canvas

All that looks golden is not gold.

African Proverbs

Artwork Title: Generations
Artwork Size: 20 x 30
Artwork Medium: Oil and Gold Leaf

As one door closes, another opens.

African Proverbs

Artwork Title: Something Else I
Artwork Size: 16 x 20
Artwork Medium: Acrylic

Worrying is like sitting in a rocking chair. It gives you something to do, but it gets you nowhere.

African Proverbs

Artwork Title: Sit and Relax
Artwork Size: 16 x 20
Artwork Medium: Acrylic

Try something new.
Enjoy Life.

Terry Tabor

Artwork Title: Giving
Artwork Size: 16 x 20
Artwork Medium: Painted on Silk

When we change our way of thinking
everything changes.

African Proverb

Artwork Title: Breathe
Artwork Size: 12 x 16
Artwork Medium: Acrylic with glass stones

When you do what you love, you are happy.
When you do what you are good at, you are at peace.

African Proverb

Artwork Title: Faces
Artwork Size: 18 x 24
Artwork Medium: Acrylic

Two wrong doesn't make it right.

African Proverb

Artwork Title: Get Along With Others
Artwork Size: 15 x 15
Artwork Medium: Painted on Silk

Enjoy the moment of being alone.
You are the best person to be with.
It's doesn't mean you are lonely.

Terry Tabor

Artwork Title: Just Relax II
Artwork Size: 15 x 15
Artwork Medium: Silk

It's best to have soup with someone you love,
Then to have steak with someone you hate.

African Proverb

Artwork Title: Just Relax Alone II
Artwork Size: 17 x 22
Artwork Medium: Acrylic

Worrying doesn't take away tomorrow's troubles;
it takes away todays' peace.

African Proverb

Artwork Title: *Music Man*
Artwork Size: *14 x 16*
Artwork Medium: *Silk*

Live each day as if it is your last.

African Proverb

Artwork Title: Name That Tune
Artwork Size: 12 x 36
Artwork Medium: Acrylic with Music Notes

That's water under the bridge.

African Proverb

Artwork Title: Forgiving
Artwork Size: 18 x 23
Artwork Medium: Acrylic

Early Bird gets the worm.

African Proverb

Artwork Title: Fly Now
Artwork Size: 10 x 12
Artwork Medium: Acrylic

Printed in the United States
by Baker & Taylor Publisher Services